Programme Management based on MSP - A Management Guide

G000155821

Other publications by Van Haren Publishing on IT-management

Van Haren Publishing specialises in publications on Best Practices, methods and standards within IT-management and management. These publications are grouped in two series: *ITSM Library* (on behalf of ITSMF Netherlands) and *Best Practice*. At the publishing date of this publication the following books are available:

ITIL:

Foundations of IT Service Management based on ITIL, (English and and in 4 translations; also as a cd-rom)
IT Service Management based on ITIL (German, French, Japanese, Russian, Spanish)
IT Service Management - een samenvatting, 2de druk, a pocket guide (Dutch)
IT Service Management - een leerboek (Dutch)

ISO/IEC 20000:

ISO/IEC 20000 - a pocket guide (English)

ISO 27001 and ISO 17799

Information Security based on ISO 27001 and ISO 17799 - a management guide (English)
Implementing Information Security based on ISO 27001 and ISO 17799 - a management guide (English)

CobiT:

IT Governance based on CobiT - a pocket guide (English, German)

IT Service CMM:

IT Service CMM - a pocket guide (English)

ASL:

ASL - a Framework for Application Management (English)
ASL - Application Services Library - a management guide (English, Dutch)

BiSL:

BiSL - a Framework for Business Management and Information management (Dutch; English edition Summer 2006)
BiSL - Business information Services Library - a management guide (Dutch; English edition Autumn 2006)

ISPL:

IT Services Procurement op basis van ISPL (Dutch)
IT Services Procurement based on ISPL - a pocket guide (English)

PRINCE2:

Project management based on PRINCE2- Edition 2005 (Dutch, English , German, due Spring 2006)

MSP:

Programme management based on MSP (Dutch, English)
Programme management based on MSP - a management guide (English)

MoR:

Risk management based on MoR - a management guide (English)

Topics & Management instruments

Metrics for IT Service Management (English)
Six Sigma for IT Management (English)

MOF/MSF:

MOF - Microsoft Operations Framework, a pocket guide (Dutch , English, French, German, Japanese)
MSF - Microsoft Solutions Framework, a pocket guide (English, German)

For a recent update on the VHP publications, see our website: www.vanharen.net.

Programme Management based on MSP

A Management Guide

Van Haren
PUBLISHING

Colophon

Title: Programme Management based on MSP - A Management Guide

Author: Jane Chittenden (Lead)

Chief Editor: Jan van Bon

Publisher: Van Haren Publishing, Zaltbommel, www.vanharen.net

ISBN: 90 77212 67 1

Print: First edition, first impression, May 2006

Layout and design: DTPresto design and layout, Zeewolde - NL

Copyright: Van Haren Publishing 2006

Printer: Wilco, Amersfoort -- NL

For any further enquiries about Van Haren Publishing, please send an e-mail to: info@vanharen.net

Aknowledgements

The Author and Chief Editor gratefully thank and acknowledge the following for their assistance in the production of this title:

Charles Fox   Core i.s.
Tom Abram   Mantix
Nick Johns   CCLRC
Patrick Mayfield   Pearce Mayfield
Martyn Clemens   HMRC (HM Revenue and Customs)
Peter Glynne   Deloitte

We are also extremely grateful to the Best Practice User Group for use of their facilities for the QA of this title.

Best Practice User Group™ is the leading support organization for users of the OGC Best Practice products, such as PRINCE2™, Managing Successful Programmes and Management of Risk. BPUG organize workshops and conferences, represent users on technical and examination boards and host the official Issues Log on our web site.
For more information please see www.usergroup.org.uk.

Contents

CHAPTER 1

Introduction

1.1 About this book

This book provides a quick reference to programme management in a handy pocket sized format.

The information in this pocketbook is based primarily on *Managing Successful Programmes*, the best practice approach developed and owned by the UK Office of Government Commerce (OGC). The pocketbook includes other sources of best practice advice on programme management published by OGC. The principles, processes and key terms described in this pocketbook are consistent with OGC's advice and guidance on programme management.

1.2 What is a programme?

OGC defines a programme as *the coordinated management of a portfolio of projects to achieve a set of business objectives.*

Programmes may take different forms in different industry sectors, although the principles of programme management are the same. There are typically four types of programme:

- a **change programme**, which coordinates and manages a group of related projects to achieve a specific business objective
- a **policy programme**, which is a change programme intended to bring about societal change (public sector specific)
- a **work programme**, which is a group of initiatives that may or may not be related but which have to be coordinated because they call on the same pool of resources
- a **series of projects** for one client, where it makes sense to coordinate projects under one programme manager. The projects may be carried out by different project teams but draw on the same pool of resources and need to coordinate the relationship with the client.

1.3 What is programme management?

Programme management is the coordination, organisation, direction and implementation of a portfolio of related projects to achieve a defined outcome and realise specified benefits. It delivers change in manageable phases (tranches) with formal review points for checking progress against plans.

Programme management is particularly suitable for delivery of change (which might be new ways of working, organisational restructure, implementing a new policy initiative. It enables the organisation to focus on outcomes - 'where we want to be' - while allowing flexibility in the route to those outcomes.

Table 1.1 shows the key programme management terms.

Key term	Explanation
Outcome	The results of introducing change, usually concerned with achieving improvements and/or changes in behaviour
Benefit	A measurable improvement resulting from an outcome
Output	The deliverables from a project that contribute to benefits
Programme	A coordinated portfolio of projects and activities that aims to achieve a set of outcomes and realise benefits
Project	A set of coordinated activities to deliver specific outputs over a specified time period within specified parameters for cost and quality
Programme owner (also known as Senior Responsible Owner and Programme Director)	The individual with personal responsibility for the success of the programme
Programme manager	The individual who manages programme delivery
Business change manager	The role responsible for benefits realisation and for managing the transition to new ways of working

Table 1.1 *Key programme management terms*

See Appendix A for a glossary of programme management terms; see Appendix B for outlines of programme documents.

1.4 Programme or project?

A project has a definite start and end point, with the aim of delivering a specific output (or outputs) within a defined timeframe. It should have a short timescale and a clear path for its delivery, with all aspects clearly defined and well understood. Its focus is on efficient delivery of outputs.

A programme has a vision of its intended end-state but may not have a clearly defined path to get there. It almost always has a much longer timescale than a project, with many aspects uncertain at the start of the programme. Its focus is on effective achievement of outcomes.

Benefits usually accrue at the end of a project, after the project has been delivered. A programme will coordinate the delivery of a number of projects and realise benefits incrementally as the programme progresses.

If a project is large scale and/or complex and/or uncertain, with a long time frame, it should be rescoped as a set of coordinated projects and managed as a programme. If a programme is short term and very clearly defined, it should be managed as a project.

Appendix C provides more detail about the differences between programmes and projects.

CHAPTER 2

Managing change with programme management

2.1 Introduction

Successful change is difficult to achieve and can be high risk. Whatever the scope of the change, it needs to be actively managed. This section outlines the main characteristics of business change and explains how programme management enables successful change.

2.2 The context of change

No organisation stands still. Changes in the business environment, changing expectations of customers and staff, advances in technology - these are only a few of the pressures that force continuing change on the organisation. Responding to these drivers for change might mean:

- change in the way that services are delivered to customers
- relocation to new premises and/or implementing new IT facilities
- a merger or restructuring into different business units
- setting up new supply chain relationships.

As soon as the organisation moves beyond very simple changes, it needs to take account of a variety of inter-related factors:

- the **business environment** - external pressures and scope for change
- the **organisation** - internal pressures for change in structure, workforce, processes etc.
- the **technology aspects** - exploiting new technology, integrating existing infrastructure, integrating with others in the supply chain.

A major challenge is to achieve the right balance between the short-term pressures for change and the longer term corporate goals.

The cultural aspects of a change initiative must never be underestimated. Change will almost always affect the organisation's culture - 'the way we work round here'. To gain people's commitment to the change - and to retain that commitment - there must be engagement and communication with stakeholders throughout the change. After transition to new ways of working, the communication must continue if the change is to succeed in the long term.

2.3 Cross-cutting change

Cross-cutting change adds to the complexities of delivering success. Where multiple organisations come together to deliver services to each other or to the public, there will need to be continuing management and coordination of the changes in all the organisations concerned. There will also be many other stakeholders external to the main partners who have an interest in the change. Issues could include:

- differences in perception about the changes required, and the respective roles of the various organisations
- different views about the new services to be offered, the target customers and business processes to be implemented
- problems related to the mandates of each organisation: what they are allowed to change and what they must or may do
- differences in culture between the organisations, which can lead to mismatches in their approaches to change
- differences in the willingness or ability of the organisations to absorb change
- differences in planning horizons.

2.4 Different types of change

The scale of the change could range from minor adjustments to radical transformation:

- localised improvements to internal processes and procedures
- major change across the organisation, such as complete restructuring or major new service offerings to customers
- transformation outside the organisation, perhaps a merger or joint venture with a group of organisations.

Figure 2.1 shows different types of change, which will affect the style of programme management. A change that is about new facilities (Figure 2.1, top left), the programme's scope will be reasonably clear and well defined. If the programme is about changing the way the organisation works (Figure 2.1, middle), there will be some ambiguity about what the changes are and how they will be delivered. Finally, where the programme is about improvements in society (Figure 2.1, bottom right), it will be driven by the desired outcome but will typically be highly uncertain and complex to define.

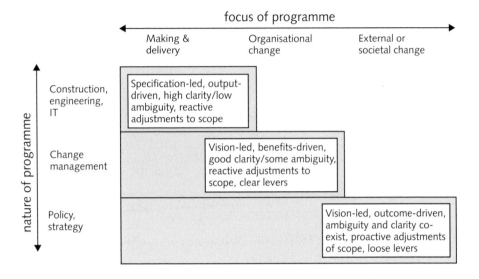

Figure 2.1 *Different types of change*

The change might be:
- **proactive**, where the organisation identifies an opportunity to do things better or in new ways
- **reactive**, in response to a crisis such as a radical shift in customer perceptions or failing a performance review.

Leadership styles will vary over the life of the programme:
- developing the vision for the future
- communicating the vision and gaining stakeholder buy-in
- acting as an enabler during implementation
- setting targets and monitoring achievement of benefits.

2.5 Summary of the change process

There are four main phases in a change initiative:
- **identifying** the type of change

- **planning** the change
- **implementing** the change
- **reviewing** the change.

Identifying the change is about determining whether it is a forced change or something that the organisation wants to do, then identifying the main considerations. These include:

- the need for the change
- stakeholders and their expectations
- the scope of the change
- the change champion who will own the change
- the key issues, which may be business, technical, political or cultural issues
- the desired outcome or outcomes.

Planning the change involves translating high level requirements into detailed action plans:

- exploring the options for achieving the change - different combinations of projects in a programme of change
- prioritising the projects that will together deliver the change
- detailed programme definition and planning.

Implementing the change is carried out in three steps:

- developing new ways of working, which may include pilots and/or new processes
- managing the transition, which may require operating the 'old' way in parallel for an interim period
- 'bedding in' new operational arrangements.

Reviewing the change is about:

- measuring success - achievement of intended outcomes and realisation of benefits
- identifying opportunities for further benefits
- learning lessons from the change initiative
- looking to the future, because change always leads to further change.

The relationship between the change phases and programme management is shown in table 2.1.

Change phase	Programme management process
1: Identifying the change	Initiating a programme
2: Planning the change	Defining a programme
3: Implementing the change	Governing a programme Managing the portfolio Managing benefits
4: Reviewing the change	Closing a programme

Table 2.1 *Relationship between change phases and programme management*

2.6 Why change initiatives fail

There has been a considerable amount of research over the last ten years into the reasons why change initiatives fail. The common causes are summarised here:
- weak leadership and senior management commitment to the change
- lack of clarity about the vision for the future
- no link to the strategic objectives of the organisation
- no sense of urgency or priority for the change
- barriers to the change not tackled
- no 'quick wins' to build early commitment to the change
- poor engagement with stakeholders
- inadequate skills in programme/project/risk management
- poor judgement on commercial aspects
- failure to manage the realisation of benefits.

2.7 How programme management enables successful change

Programme management is designed to manage uncertainty, which is inherent in change. There could be uncertainty about the path to deliver the vision or about the vision itself. Programme management manages and controls change in a volatile environment.

Programme management increases the chances of successful change through:
- realistic delivery planning - breaking delivery down into tranches that can be easily controlled
- focus on outcomes - with a clearly defined vision of the change, underpinned by a clear definition of outcomes

- focus on benefits realisation - identification of measurable benefits that are actively managed by a Business Change Manager
- a change champion - the programme's owner is personally responsible for its success
- engaging with key stakeholders in two way communication throughout the change process
- managing the transition to new ways of working - addressing cultural issues and scheduling each aspect of the change to minimise disruption to 'business as usual'.

CHAPTER 3

Programme organisation

3.1 Introduction

Programme organisation is the task of defining roles, responsibilities and reporting arrangements in such a way that everyone knows what they have to do and when. This section of the pocketbook describes the main roles and reporting structures.

Every programme is different and the capabilities available to be involved in the programme will vary. The principles of programme organisation and roles outlined in this section will need to be tailored to the needs of your organisation and specific programmes.

3.2 Leadership

The leadership role is critical to success - the programme must be directed by the right person with personal commitment to its success and the authority to make things happen.

The key principles for effective leadership of a programme are:
- the authority to make **decisions** and commit resources throughout the life of the programme
- visible **commitment** and a high profile to obtain stakeholder buy-in
- focus on the **outcomes** that meet strategic objectives for the business
- genuine understanding of the **cultural** issues and potential barriers to change
- the ability to lead the **transition** to new ways of working.

3.3 Programme organisation

Figure 3.1 shows the relationships between the main roles - the Sponsoring Group (commissioning the programme), the programme's owner (leading and directing), the Programme Manager (leading the programme team), the Business Change Manager (making the change happen according to plan) and the Programme Office (coordinating activities and information).

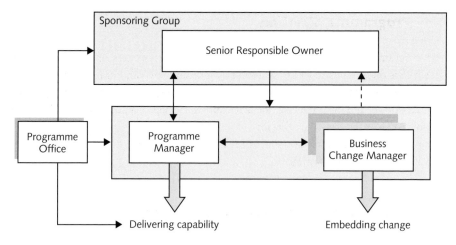

Figure 3.1 *Basic programme organisation*

3.4 Programme sponsorship

The programme's sponsors identify the need for the programme and make the investment decision to go ahead with it (a commitment to resources - funding and people). The sponsors are usually a group rather than an individual (for example, the management board). The Sponsoring Group will ensure senior management commitment and support throughout the programme's life.

The key stakeholders make up the Sponsoring Group for the programme.

The main responsibilities of the Sponsoring Group include:
* identifying the need for the programme (the Programme Mandate) and committing to resources (the investment decision)
* appointing the programme owner and providing ongoing support to that role
* approving the progress of the programme at agreed milestones against the strategic objectives
* engaging with the stakeholders represented by each member of the Sponsoring Group, to obtain their commitment to the programme
* confirming at programme closure that the programme's objectives have been achieved.

3.5 Programme direction

The programme owner has overall accountability for the success of the programme. This role is often referred to as the Senior Responsible Owner, because the individual must be senior enough to have authority, take personal responsibility for the programme as its champion and ownership of the achievement of objectives and benefits. The role is also known as Programme Director.

This person should be a senior member of the Sponsoring Group, with the authority to lead and direct the programme.

3.6 Day-to-day programme management

The Programme Manager is responsible, on behalf of the programme owner, for successful delivery of the programme.

The Programme Manager plans and coordinates the projects within the programme, keeping track of interdependencies between the projects and any changes that could affect success. He/she manages the issues and risks from a programme perspective, taking corrective action as appropriate. An important part of this role is defining the programme's governance framework - responsibilities and reporting arrangements across the programme, coordinating reporting from the individual projects. The Programme Manager will also manage stakeholder communications and the programme's budgets, allocating resources as required.

Day-to-day management of the projects is carried out by their respective project managers.

3.7 Delivery of business change

The role of the Business Change Manager, on behalf of the programme owner, is focused on benefits realisation, ensuring that the Sponsoring Group's objectives are met. This role must be located in the business, providing a bridge between the business and the programme. The Business Change Manager role ensures a smooth transition to new ways of working and subsequently identifies opportunities for further benefits to be achieved. There is only one Business Change Manager role in a programme; however, there may be multiple people performing the role on behalf of different parts of the business.

Change may affect different parts of the organisation. For a major change initiative there should be an individual contributing to the Business Change Manager role for each business area affected by the change.

3.8 Supporting the programme

The Programme Office (also known as the Programme Support Office) coordinates all the programme's information, communication, monitoring and control activities.

The main tasks are:
- tracking and reporting on progress overall and of individual projects within the programme, including reporting on risks and issues
- managing the programme's information (in a large programme, there will be a substantial library of documents that will require constant updating)
- supporting the Programme Manager in managing the programme budget
- managing the quality aspects (fitness for purpose of deliverables)
- change control (keeping track of actions taken that could change the programme's direction).

The level of resourcing for the Programme Office will vary depending on the size and capabilities of the organisation. It may be required to coordinate a number of programmes. In the UK central government this coordinating function is known as a centre of excellence; another widely used term is Programme Management Office.

3.9 Designing and implementing a programme organisation

Programme organisation defines the key roles and responsibilities in a ways that is clearly understood by everyone involved. It is important to separate the roles of the Sponsoring Group (making the investment decision), programme owner (leading and directing the programme) and the Programme Manager (leading the programme team and coordinating projects within the programme). These roles should never be combined because there could be conflicts of interest. All other roles can be combined.
Reporting lines should be kept short, to facilitate efficient communication across the programme. A good reporting structure ensures that there are no conflicting instructions (a common cause of programme failure).

The programme organisation must be tailored to the requirements of a specific programme. It takes account of:

- the relationship required with project organisations - there must be clear reporting lines from the individual projects, through a project board if required
- whether responsibilities need to be assigned to more than one individual (large-scale programmes) or combined (smaller organisations and/or smaller programmes)
- managing cross-organisational roles, where several organisations are working in partnership
- whether a formal Programme Board is needed, in which case the programme owner would chair the board as its executive and key stakeholders take the role of Programme Board members.

Figure 3.2 shows the relationship between programme and project organisations.

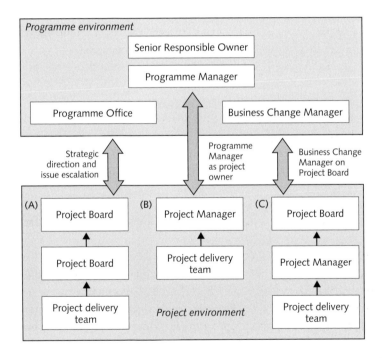

Figure 3.2 *Programme and project organisations*

3.10 Cross-organisational programmes

For cross-organisational programmes, each participating organisation should have a clearly defined role that is agreed and understood by all; there must be no uncertainty about who is responsible for what. Complexity can occur where there are multiple budget holders or where one party provides funding and another obtains the benefits, for example. It may be appropriate to set up a completely separate entity for the life of the programme to deal with any potential conflicts of interest between the group as a whole and its constituent parts.

Some key success factors include:
- defining goals that are valued by all parties
- collectively assessing progress and taking collective responsibility for action when required
- committing to adequate resources, ideally from a shared budget
- effective leadership by the programme owner - which may be a challenge where some of the participating organisations are outside their control.

3.11 Human Resource considerations

The programme team needs to be adequately resourced, with people released from their 'day jobs' and normal line management arrangements. HR policies may need to be drawn up covering the arrangements between staff on the programme team and others in the organisation(s).

3.12 Procurement considerations

Many programmes require procurement - for example, to acquire new IT, training or consultancy support. The central procurement unit (or equivalent function) will need to provide procurement expertise and/or advise on procurement activities, including contract management after the change has taken place.

CHAPTER 4

Benefits management

4.1 Introduction

A benefit is an advantage or gain. In the context of programme management benefits are the measurable results of achieving a programme's desired outcome. Benefits management is the activity that defines outcomes in measurable terms and checks that they are being achieved.

The programme's Business Case provides justification for the investment it will require. Benefits management works alongside this, enabling the programme to plan for and achieve benefits. It also works closely with stakeholder communications, because stakeholders will be affected by benefits realisation.

4.2 The benefits management process

The benefits management process starts with the description of the required outcomes, then defines a framework for the benefits management and realisation. This will include:

- developing a Benefits Management Strategy that sets out the roles and responsibilities and actions required from management as the owners of the benefits
- translating the desired outcomes into benefits and dis-benefits (negative impact of introducing the change)
- modelling the benefits (and dis-benefits) to determine the sequences of their delivery and dependencies
- defining and quantifying the benefits in detail in Benefit Profiles
- planning how the benefits will be realised and measured
- reviewing the realisation of benefits against the strategy
- examining the business environment for factors that may limit or improve opportunities for further benefits.

4.3 The Benefits Management Strategy

The Benefits Management Strategy defines the delivery framework for achieving the programme's strategic objectives. It determines how individual benefits will be measured, how the overall set of benefits will be assessed and their progress tracked, and the management actions required to realise the benefits.

An effective Benefits Management Strategy demonstrates that:
• the overall set of benefits matches the required outcomes defined in the Business Case
• stakeholders have been adequately consulted and are committed
• the necessary resources will be made available to deliver the strategy
• responsibilities for benefits management have been identified and allocated, especially the Business Change Manager
• the strategy is integrated with other programme plans and strategies.

Dis-benefits are the negative outcomes from change, such as increased costs or additional skills required as a result of implementing the change. They should be treated in exactly the same way as benefits.

Each benefit should be owned by an appropriate senior manager in the business. This ensures that there is accountability for achievement of benefits in the business area affected by the change. Ultimately, all benefits are owned by the programme owner.

4.4 Quantifying benefits

Benefits should be quantified and measured in monetary terms wherever possible. For example, there are standard figures for the cost of a person's time, which enables the organisation to place some value on the cost of time saved. However, if this is not possible, there should be some sort of numerical value - for example, a reduction of x minutes in processing a claim.

Some benefits are notoriously difficult to quantify, such as measures of customer satisfaction. However, it is important to note that if a benefit cannot be measured it cannot be tracked and the benefit's owner will not know whether it has been achieved.

4.5   Benefit Profiles

A Benefits Profile provides a full description of a benefit including details of the measures, ownership responsibilities, links, and dependencies, costs associated with realisation and measures and the time over which the benefit will be realised. Every benefit needs to be fully defined to enable the programme to track and monitor their progress.

When developing the Benefits Profiles, the relationships between benefits are established, together with a clear understanding of what needs to be in place for a benefit to happen and how it fits into the overall picture of change. Both short and long-term benefits need to be considered to ensure continued focus and commitment to the programme. See Appendix B for a Benefit Profile template.

Figure 4.1 shows a high level view of the relationships between benefits.

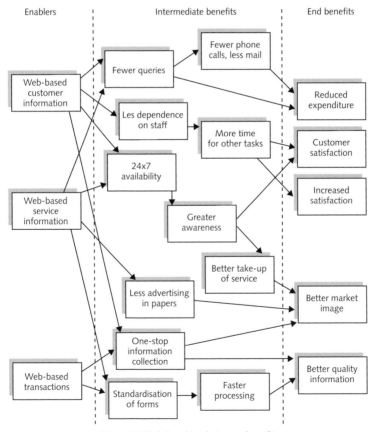

Figure 4.1 *Relationships between benefits*

4.6   The Benefits Realisation Plan

The Benefits Realisation Plan provides an overview of all the Benefits Profiles, defining when each benefit or group of benefits will be achieved and any management activity that is required to make it happen - such as reorganising the work of a team or providing training. These 'people' aspects can have a significant impact on the success of the change and should never be underestimated.

4.7   Reviewing benefit realisation

The objectives of benefit reviews are:
- to assess and update the Benefit Profiles and Benefits Realisation Plan to check that progress is proceeding according to plan
- to check that the overall set of benefits remains consistent with the programme's strategic direction
- to keep stakeholders informed about progress, especially 'quick wins'
- to assess how well the new ways of working perform in comparison with their original (baseline) performance levels
- to review the effectiveness of benefits management so that lessons can be learned for the future.

4.8   Responsibilities for benefits management

Benefits management is ultimately the responsibility of the whole programme management team and many of the programme's stakeholders. However, the key to benefits realisation is to establish clear individual ownership of benefits. The main role in benefits management is the Business Change Manager role, liaising with senior managers in the affected business areas and reporting to the programme owner.

CHAPTER 5

Stakeholder management and communications

5.1 Introduction

The programme's stakeholders include anyone who is working on or contributing to the programme as well as those who may be affected by the programme. Stakeholders will support the change to varying degrees; some will champion the change and some will actively resist it. Some stakeholders need to be actively engaged; others merely need to be kept informed. Stakeholder management is concerned with all of these issues.

5.2 Identifying stakeholders

The programme's Vision Statement and Blueprint (the description of what the organisation will look like after the change) provide the starting point for identifying the stakeholders and what they want from the programme.

Stakeholders can be grouped under categories such as those who have a governance role, those who will influence success, those who will benefit and those who will oppose the change. A Stakeholder Map defines the key stakeholders in relation to their interests in the programme. Another widely used technique is a RACI analysis, which identifies which stakeholders are Responsible, which are Accountable, which should be Consulted and which should just be Informed.

It may be critically important to understand the needs of different customer groups - perhaps because the organisation has to make choices about multiple channels for delivering new services to its customer base. Customer segmentation techniques are very useful in defining the characteristics of each customer group and hence their needs.

Figure 5.1 shows typical groups of stakeholders.

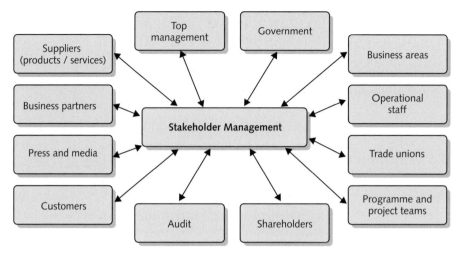

Figure 5.1 *Typical groups of stakeholders*

5.3 Stakeholder Management Strategy

The Stakeholder Management Strategy addresses these key questions:
* **who** are the stakeholders and how are they grouped?
* **what** are their interests and likely influences?
* **how** will the programme engage with them?
* **what** information will be communicated to each stakeholder group and when?
* **how** will feedback be obtained and used?

5.4 Stakeholder communication

The objectives of stakeholder communication are to:
* maintain awareness and commitment - stakeholder buy-in
* publish consistent messages about the programme
* manage stakeholder expectations.

Some key questions to ask about stakeholder communication include:
* are the key messages clear and easy to understand?
* are we getting the right messages through to each of our target stakeholder groups?

- are we collecting useful feedback from stakeholders?
- are we demonstrating that we are responding to this feedback?

5.5   The Communications Plan

The Communications Plan should be defined and implemented as early as possible and then maintained throughout the programme. It should identify the key communication channels, the objectives to be met (for example, publicising success or breaking down barriers), the key messages and the stakeholders to be reached. It defines in detail what information to be communicated, when and how (which channels will be used, such as press coverage and/or open days); it includes how two-way communication will be achieved such as responses to stakeholder concerns about the change.

Checklist for engaging with stakeholders:
- does everyone involved understand what is meant by 'stakeholder'?
- have stakeholders been segmented into relevant groups that are being targeted in relation to their specific interests?
- does the Communications Plan reflect the requirements of these groups?
- is there evidence that key stakeholder groups are actively engaged in the programme and feel that their concerns are being listened to?

5.6   Responsibilities for stakeholder management

Development and implementation of the Stakeholder Management Strategy and Communication Plan is the responsibility of the Programme Manager.
The Programme Office maintains the information about stakeholders. It facilitates implementation of the Communications Plan and checks that its activities are happening according to plan; it also captures any issues that are raised in stakeholder consultation and feeds these into programme planning.

CHAPTER 6

Risk management and issue resolution

6.1 Introduction

Change is inherently risky because of uncertainties about outcomes. Major change programmes may be volatile, complex and at any time subject to unexpected change in direction. Programme management has to manage all of the risks and issues that may arise in the programme management environment.

Risks are things that may happen in the future, which may be positive opportunity or negative threat. Threats are factors that could lead to risks occurring - that is, they will be the cause of a risk. Issues are things happening now that could cause problems for the programme.

Risk management is concerned with keeping the programme's exposure to risk at an acceptable level. The task of issue resolution is to prevent an issue from threatening the programme's chances of achieving its objectives.

Risk management and issue resolution need to be formally incorporated at the project level within a programme. It is important to understand that risks and issues cannot always be contained at project level. A major issue facing a particular project could undermine the whole programme if left unchecked.

6.2 Risk management overview

Risk management involves:
- processes to track the current status of risks
- timely and accurate reporting on risks
- taking prompt action to mitigate risks
- follow up to check that these actions have been effective.

Figure 6.1 shows risk management in overview.

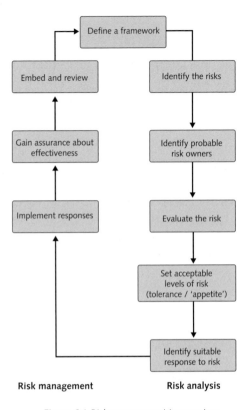

Figure 6.1 *Risk management in overview*

6.3   The Risk Management Strategy

The Risk Management Strategy is a document setting the context in which risks will be identified, allocated to owners, analysed, acted upon, monitored and reviewed.

It defines processes for:
- identifying and quantifying risks
- assessing the likelihood of their occurring (probability) and impact
- ownership of individual risks
- making decisions about risk
- reviewing for effectiveness
- engaging with stakeholders on risk aspects.

6.4   Risk identification

Risk identification means establishing exactly what is at risk - for example, agreed activities cannot be completed within the planned timeframe or budgets are at risk of being overrun. Risks are identified early in the programme, when choices are being made about the optimum balance of cost, benefit and risk. Trade-offs are made between:

- **cost** - how affordable?
- **benefit** - how valuable / useful would this be in meeting business objectives?
- **risk** - how complex / uncertain / ambitious in scale?

Risk identification continues throughout the life of the programme. Risks should be documented in the programme's Risk Register. This captures and cooordinates information about the risks across the programme and provides the basis for prioritisation, action, control and reporting. The Risk Register must be continually updated and reviewed throughout the programme's life.

The main categories of risk are:

- strategic - typically, external factors that could force a change in strategic direction
- programme level - where assumptions or interdependencies between projects change, putting benefits realisation at risk
- project level - typically time and cost overruns
- operational risks - often at the point of handover to new ways of working.

6.5   Risk ownership and allocation

The Programme Manager is responsible for ensuring that all risks are owned at the appropriate level. Each identified risk should be allocated to the individual who is best placed to deal with it - for example, a supplier or a manager in the affected business unit. For major programmes there may be a dedicated Risk Manager role, where the person appointed has specialist expertise in risk management.

6.6   Risk evaluation

Risk evaluation means assessing the probability of the risk occurring and the potential impact if it occurs. From a programme perspective, it is important to consider the total level of risk as well as individual risks, to check whether an unacceptable level of risk has been reached overall.

6.7   Responses to risk

These can be summarised as 'the four Ts':
- **Transfer** the risk to the party best placed to manage it
- **Tolerate** the risk - the 'do nothing' option, which means the programme will accept the consequences of the risk happening.
- **Terminate** the risk by rescoping the programme to remove the risk
- **Treat** the risk by taking corrective actions to reduce the probability or impact of the risk.

6.8   Implementing actions and reporting on risk

There will be a cost implication in managing risk - for example, allowing for a longer development time for a new IT system. The costs should be accounted for separately from the main programme budget as a set of risk allowances for each project.

The risk allowance is estimated on the costs of the maximum and minimum risks likely to occur; the average risk between the two extremes is then used as the basis of the risk allowance. In the early project stages, the risk allowance for each element may be greater than the estimate for the project budget. As each project in the programme develops and becomes more clearly defined, funding is spent on investigations, feasibility studies, etc. The risk allowance is steadily reduced as the risks or their consequences are minimised by good risk management and required funds are transferred to the main programme budget to cover the costs of risks. At the same time the estimate for the project budget will steadily increase as risks materialise.

Risk allowances should be reviewed regularly through the life of each project, and appropriate adjustments made to the project estimate and risk allowance depending on the risks materialising or not.

Risk actions should be planned, resourced and implemented. Stakeholders should be kept informed, especially if they are directly affected.

Project-specific risks are managed at the project level, with monthly reporting (or as required) coordinated by the Programme Office. It is important to set consistent criteria for assessing and reporting on risks across the programme. A useful way to show the aggregated risk situation is to categorise risks as Red (must take immediate action); Amber (proceed with caution) and Green (progressing without problems) and then to plot the position of these risks on a matrix that indicates their strategic importance. At a glance, senior managers can then see whether the overall exposure to risk is becoming unacceptable.

6.9 Assurance and effectiveness of risk management

Risk management processes should be assessed to determine how well risks have been managed, whether the key risks have actually been identified and how effectively they were treated.

6.10 Issue management

An issue may be:
- a risk that has materialised and needs to be managed
- a required change to the programme
- a problem affecting the programme.

Issues need to be managed in the same way as risks and captured in an Issues Log. Regular reporting on individual issues and their overall impact is done in the same way as for risk management. They should be prioritised in terms of their actual or potential affect on the programme.
Cross-programme issues should be captured and formally assessed in terms of their impact on the programme.

6.11 The Issue Resolution Strategy

The Issue Resolution Strategy sets out how issues are captured and assessed before action is taken to resolve them. It defines processes for:
- collecting information for issue assessment
- assessing and prioritising issues
- allocating issue owners and responsibilities for resolving issues.

All issues raised during the life of the programme should be captured and tracked in the programme's Issue Log. Issues that are future concerns rather than current problems should be managed as risks in the Risk Register.
Cross-programme issues should be given a high priority. These issues have an impact across the programme and/or more than one programme. Because of their high priority these issues usually need to be escalated to top management.

6.12 Change control

Where there is a change, whether a major rescope or a minor adjustment, its impact on the programme needs to be understood. Procedures for change control should take account of:

- how information is captured in the Issues Log and audit trail
- how potential changes will be prioritised
- how the impact of the change and its associated risks will be assessed against the Business Case, Programme Plan etc.
- how the priority status will be re-evaluated
- how to decide which changes to accommodate
- how to implement the approved changes and inform the relevant stakeholders.

6.13 Integration between the programme and its projects

Project-level issues and risks should be escalated to the programme level, when required; conversely, programme-level risks may need to descend to project level. Programme Managers and Business Change Managers need to have visibility of cross-project and higher level risks and issues, to ensure that they are clearly understood, together with their wider implications to other projects and the programme itself.

It is important that all project teams have a shared understanding of the change control process.

6.14 Responsibilities for risk management and issue resolution

The programme owner is responsible for ensuring that risks and issues are managed effectively, with key strategic risks and issues escalated to senior management and acted upon. For major programmes, there should be a Risk Manager dedicated to the task. The Programme Office manages and coordinates support for risk and issue management.

CHAPTER 7

Programme planning and control

7.1 Introduction

Programme planning and control brings together project planning and monitoring as a coherent programme activity. This section describes how all the elements of programme planning and control are coordinated through the Programme Plan.

The relationship between the elements of programme planning, and the central Programme Plan, is shown in Figure 7.1.

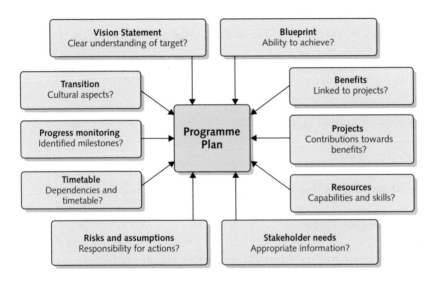

Figure 7.1 *Contributions to programme planning and control*

The inputs to programme planning and control are:
- the Vision Statement, which describes the future state - new ways of working. It provides one of the early inputs to programme planning by setting out the outcome(s) the programme is aiming to achieve

- the Blueprint, which is a model of the future business or organisation. It covers working practices and processes, as well as the information and technology it needs to achieve the aims set out in the Vision Statement.
- details of the benefits to be realised - the Benefits Realisation Plan and the Benefits Profiles set out the programme's benefits
- details of the projects in the Project Portfolio, both current and planned
- the resources required (people, buildings, funding etc) including resources to be shared between projects
- the main stakeholders and plans for communicating with each stakeholder group
- the main risks and plans for managing them
- the timetable, including planned milestones
- how progress will be monitored
- plans for the transition to new ways of working.

7.2   Planning and scheduling

Programme planning is concerned with deciding exactly what is to be done, who will do it and so on. It is an ongoing activity throughout the life of the programme.

The key steps in the planning process include:
- deciding on the projects in the Project Portfolio
- a timetable for project delivery, demonstrating realisation of benefits alongside strategic objectives
- the development of more detailed project plans
- responding to issues as and when they arise
- continual monitoring and review of projects to ensure they meet the overall objectives of the programme.

The Project Portfolio sets out the individual projects needed by the programme. Each will have its own plan and timetable and its co-ordination with other projects as well as its overall contribution to the programme.

A dependency network model is a useful way of identifying the relationship between the projects.

The programme schedule should be divided into groups of projects (tranches) and milestones for programme review, linked to the delivery of benefits. Some projects will overlap between tranches; some will be new projects and some will be closing at the end of a tranche. Figure 7.2 shows an example programme schedule.

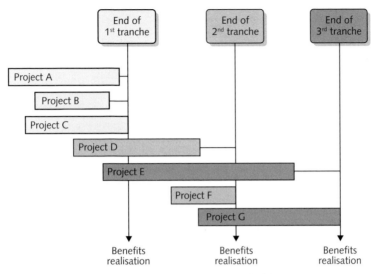

Figure 7.2 *Example programme schedule*

Prioritisation will affect programme scheduling; it must focus on essential programme activities. Trade-offs may have to be made between competing projects or resources, for example.

7.3 Managing resources

Programme planning must include required resources, which will include:
- the programme's financial aspects
- human resources and stakeholders
- the physical assets of the programme including buildings and equipment, for example
- the IT and infrastructure the programme will rely on to deliver its objectives.

The Resource Management Strategy describes how resources are to be acquired, used and disposed of throughout the programme and its Project Portfolio, to ensure efficient and effective use of resources.

7.4   Programme-level control

Programme level control is a two-way process - providing relevant planning information to projects and obtaining accurate, timely information from the projects to inform management decisions about the programme.

In order to control the programme's projects effectively, individuals must have sufficient experience of project management and the experience to keep risks at a tolerable level. It is important that information is shared across the Project Portfolio, implementing common reporting standards through clear communication.

Each project should have its own individual process for its management. However, project-level governance must ensure that projects remain consistent with the objectives of the programme. The Business Cases for the projects should have a clear statement of their objectives, which should show their contribution to strategic objectives.

The programme level must be aware of the risks, issues and interdependencies across the Project Portfolio, in order to identify their (potential) impact on the programme as a whole.

7.5   Integration of information

It is essential to share information so that:
- both the project and the programme level are aware of any strategic changes, for example to the Blueprint
- there is awareness of responsibilities and ownership of any risks and issues that are managed at the programme level but may affect individual projects
- limits are set for costs, quality and timescales at the project level
- project-level milestones and review points are integrated.

7.6   Progress monitoring and performance measurement

The Programme Plan tracks every activity that affects programme success. It has to be timely, accurate and always up-to-date, responding to changes as they occur.

It is the purpose of the Programme Plan to identify projects or activities that are critical to the success of the programme. In order to do this, performance measures should be: Specific, Measurable, Achievable, Relevant and Timed (SMART), to give a balanced picture of the programme.

7.7   The Programme Plan

The Programme Plan is the key document for controlling programme delivery. It should include:

- project timescales for each project in the Project Portfolio, costs, outputs and dependencies
- the main risks and assumptions
- a schedule showing the programme's tranches
- the transition plan
- monitoring and control activities
- performance targets and measures.

Developing the Programme Plan will require an understanding of:

- the level of detail required to provide enough information and be a useful tool for highlighting any potential pitfalls along the way
- the tools that will be used to maintain and monitor the Programme Plan
- how this information will be communicated to stakeholders and when
- how project-level information will incorporated into the programme level.

7.8   Responsibilities for programme planning and control

Approval of the Programme Plan is the responsibility of the programme owner.

Responsibility for design and implementation of the Programme Plan lies with the Programme Manager.

Transition is the responsibility of the Business Change Manager role, which will need to provide key input to the Programme Plan on these aspects.

The Programme Office supports the Programme Manager in developing and implementing planning and control activities.

CHAPTER 8

Business Case management

8.1 Introduction

The Business Case describes why the programme is required, its value to the organisation, the benefits, costs and risks. It is important to note that the Business Case is not just about obtaining funding; it must demonstrate a clear link to strategic objectives. There will be Business Cases for each of the projects, similarly linked to the programme Business Case. This section describes how the Business Case is developed and updated.

8.2 The starting point of the Business Case

For a programme to start, the organisation's senior managers must define and agree the policies or strategies that make up the strategic direction for the organisation. This will include an exploration of how strategies will be delivered, and an assessment of priorities.

A successful outcome can only be achieved through a realistic examination of the organisation's ability to drive through the changes that need to be made.

The Programme Mandate is a statement from the Sponsoring Group that the programme is required. It initiates programme start-up, highlighting the strategic objectives for the programme and the improvements that are expected from the proposed change.

8.3 Development of the Business Case

The Business Case is critically important as it demonstrates strategic fit - that is, why the programme is needed at all. It explores potential options for delivery and makes trade-offs on the basis of current priorities and capability to deliver the change. It sets out the costs that will be incurred by the programme and provides a cost-benefit analysis of the programme, highlighting the realisation of benefits and the value of these benefits to the organisation. It identifies the risks to a successful outcome, such as poor customer take-up of a new service or uncertainty about a new technology, and proposes ways of managing those risks. It balances the costs, benefits and risks in the light of the organisation's current priorities and capability to establish the viability of the programme.

The Business Case is developed in several iterations, starting with a high level strategic outline. It is gradually refined as more information becomes available from the projects, whose Business Cases are developed to a much more detailed level.

The Business Case must be challenged at programme reviews to confirm the programme's continued viability. The Business Case should be kept up to date in order to ensure the benefits are being delivered and that the anticipated changes are being made.

8.4   Reviewing the Business Case

Reviewing the Business Case should provide answers to the following questions:
- is the programme (still) affordable?
- is the outcome (still) achievable?
- does the programme (still) demonstrate value for money?
- have all the options been considered?

8.5   Managing the Business Case

The Business Case must be flexible and adaptable to the changing business environment and priorities as well as the change itself. The Business Case must be able to identify these changes to ensure the programme stays on track to achieve its strategic objectives.

8.6   Responsibilities for Business Case management

The Business Case is the responsibility of the programme owner, who must account for it to the Sponsoring Group. The programme owner ensures that the Business Case is kept up to date, is based on the evidence of similar programmes wherever possible and continues to be aligned to strategic objectives.

For cross cutting programmes, it may be difficult to determine the individual who should 'own' the Business Case. Typically the major budget holder is assigned ownership, but not always.

The programme team and Programme Office will be involved in providing detailed information; specialist information may be required - for example, from financial advisers.

The Business Change Manager is responsible for benefits definition in the Business Case.

CHAPTER 9

Quality management

9.1 Introduction

Quality should be a top priority for the programme. It includes the quality of leadership, of its deliverables (their fitness for purpose) and of its performance management activities. It is a continuous activity that brings together configuration management, quality assurance, quality management of governance arrangements and compliance with industry standards and best practice. This section outlines the main quality aspects, which should all feature in the Quality Management Strategy.

9.2 Configuration Management

Configuration Management is about making sure that all of the individual parts of the process are working well together and moving in the same direction, after formal approvals.

Configuration Management identifies, protects and tracks all of the programme's assets and deliverables. It ensures consistency and coherency of these items to the benefit of the programme.

The assets and deliverables (products) of a programme are known as Configuration Items (CIs). Each CI must be independently identified.

Configuration Management involves:

- **planning**: what degree of Configuration Management is needed for the programme and how this level will be achieved
- **identification**: identifying all the CIs that will be useful to the programme
- **control**: establishing when individual products or complete configurations will be agreed and 'frozen' ('baselined') so that future changes are only made with appropriate levels of agreement and approval
- **reporting**: providing all the relevant information about each product and configuration
- **reviewing**: ensuring consistency between the products and configuration.

Configuration Management is also needed at the project level.

Individuals with appropriate experience and authority will be responsible for approving and reviewing the CIs.

Programme auditors should assist the Programme Manager with specific audit requirements for the programme.

9.3 Assessing quality

The programme's management processes must be capable of demonstrating:
- the effectiveness of its governance arrangements
- stakeholder needs are being met
- the investment in business change is achieving the required outcomes.

Quality reviews are integral aspect of programme reviews, which are typically scheduled at the end of a tranche when a package of benefits is achieved and/or a group of projects is brought to a close.

9.4 Audit reviews

Audit reviews check that the programme's management complies with internal standards, which may include codes of practice, accounting standards etc.

Programme audits (internal or external) scrutinise such aspects as risk management, engagement with stakeholders and contingency arrangements in case of disaster.

9.5 Programme assurance

Programme assurance demonstrates that the programme is being managed well. It may investigate:
- **quality management** (whether the deliverables are fit for purpose in general terms)
- **business assurance** (whether the deliverables meet the needs of the business)
- **stakeholder assurance** (whether the deliverables meet the needs of stakeholders).

The programme should provide continual assurance to the Programme Manager regarding the effectiveness of risk management strategies and to the Business Change Manager on issues affecting stakeholders, so that they are dealt with appropriately.

Programme governance should consider:

- what needs to be assured (management processes, stakeholder requirements, for example)?
- what skills and experience are needed to carry out the required assurance?
- how and when will assurance be undertaken for the projects and the whole programme?
- what outputs will the assurance function need to provide?
- how will the assurance function keep up to date with changes to the programme?

Project assurance is the responsibility of individual projects.

9.6 The Quality Management Strategy

The Quality Management Strategy sets out how quality will be assessed within the programme, **who** will be responsible for carrying out quality activities, and **how** the programme will comply with the required standards of quality for the organisation.

The programme owner has ultimate accountability for programme quality. The Programme Manager is responsible for the Quality Management Strategy. The benefits realised from these outputs are the responsibility of the Business Change Manager.

CHAPTER 10

Overview of processes and products

10.1 Introduction

This section provides an overview of the programme management processes and key deliverables (products). Figure 10.1 shows how these are related. It shows a linear progression, although in practice a process may have several iterations before the next one can begin; or a change in strategic direction might mean that an earlier process is revisited.

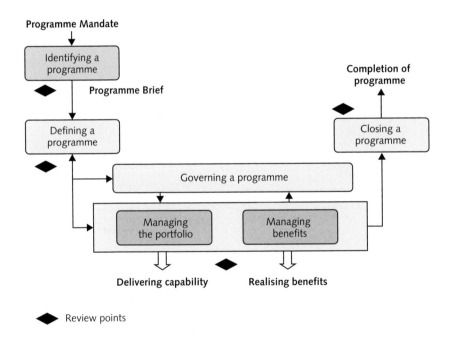

Figure 10.1 *Programme management processes and key deliverables*

10.2 Programme information

Programme information is the collection of information that:
- defines what the programme will deliver
- how it will deliver
- what the expected benefits will be
- who will be involved
- the financial implications.

Figure 10.2 shows the relationships between the main programme information sources.

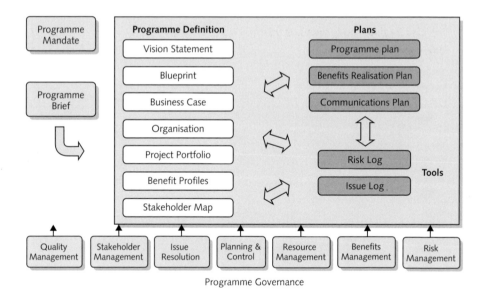

Figure 10.2 *Relationships between programme information sources*

The Programme Brief is the starting point for programme definition, which defines what the programme is intended to deliver, what benefits will be achieved, who will do the work and how they will do it, and what it will cost.

Programme governance is drawn together from a number of sources, which include:
- **programme organisation** (roles, responsibilities and reporting arrangements)
- **quality** (responsibilities for business and stakeholder assurance)

- **stakeholder assessment** (those stakeholders who are responsible and/or accountable)
- **issues and risks** (their owners and the management activities that they must carry out)
- **benefits** (their owners and the benefits realisation activities that they must carry out)
- **resources** (budget holders and others who have committed resources).

Plans are managed through:
- the **Programme Plan** (the focal point for all programme planning information)
- the **Benefits Realisation Plan** (detailing which benefits, how they will be managed and who is involved)
- the **Communications Plan** (describing how the programme will engage with stakeholders)
- the **Risk Register and Issue Log** (capturing and recording the status of current risks and issues).

CHAPTER 11

Identifying a programme

11.1 Introduction

Identifying a programme begins when a response is made to a driver for change. It is a short sharply focused process, typically only a few weeks in duration.

This section describes how the programme is identified at a high level as the basis for a go/no go management decision on whether to proceed.

11.2 Sponsoring the programme and confirming the Programme Mandate

The Sponsoring Group provides the Programme Mandate, which sets out the strategic objectives for the programme. It is not necessarily a single document; it may be a collection of documents or even just the minutes of a management meeting. The important point is that it is a statement of strategic intent in some documented form. The Sponsoring Group confirms its acceptance of the Mandate and their individual roles in the programme, then appoints the programme owner. This individual will be the champion for the programme and should be appointed as soon as possible to provide leadership and direction.

11.3 Producing the Programme Brief

The programme owner is responsible for developing the Programme Brief, with support from a small team as required. The Programme Brief is the major input to *Defining a programme*; it provides the foundation for the programme definition, as well as the plans and strategies for programme governance. The outline Vision Statement is a key input to the Programme Brief.

The objectives from the Programme Mandate are incorporated into the Programme Brief, which is formally approved by the Sponsoring Group and the programme owner; then the programme can proceed.

The expected benefits, risks, costs and timescales will need to be established with reasonable accuracy, to provide enough information to support the management decision to decide whether to go ahead with *Defining a programme*.

11.4 Developing terms of reference for programme definition

The next process, *Defining a programme*, involves detailed scoping and planning. It is critical to plan efficiently and effectively in terms of sufficient time and resources and the right people, in order to develop a programme definition. There will be a lot of uncertainty and ambiguity at this early stage, which can be greatly reduced by effective planning.

11.5 Review

Formal reviews should be put in place to establish whether the organisation has the capability and capacity to deliver its objectives and realise the benefits. This could be an internal review by a peer group in the organisation or an external review. Whether internal or external, the review team should be independent of the programme to enable an objective view of the programme's likelihood of success.

11.6 Approval to proceed

In order to proceed to *Defining a programme*, there must be clear justification for the investment of resources for the programme, and there must be sufficient evidence to indicate that the benefits will outweigh the risks.

Summary of programme information for this process	
Programme Mandate	confirmed
Programme Brief	created
Vision Statement	created

Table 11.1 *Summary of programme information for* Identifying a programme

CHAPTER 12

Defining a programme

12.1 Introduction

Defining a programme involves detailed scoping and planning; it provides the basis for deciding whether to go ahead with the programme. The main activities in this process are:

- establishing the **initial programme team** to define the programme
- developing the **Vision Statement**.

This section outlines the key activities to inform the go/no go decision.

12.2 Developing the Vision Statement

The Vision Statement sets out the desired outcomes and provides the foundation for stakeholder communication. The information from the Programme Brief is then incorporated into the Vision statement.

12.3 Developing the Blueprint

Designing the Blueprint to realise the required benefits needs to be balanced against the costs of realising those benefits. The programme's Business Case is developed in parallel with the Blueprint to ensure consistency between the proposed changes to the organisation, the costs of making the changes, and realistic realisation of the benefits required.

12.4 Defining the benefits

The Benefits Profiles give a complete definition of each benefit or dis-benefit associated with the programme. Each Benefit Profile must include:

- a description of the benefit
- its relationship to other benefits

- when it is be realised
- measures and performance indicators used to assess achievement levels and their costs
- what elements of the Blueprint are needed in order for the benefit to be realised
- which project(s) or activity is related to realisation of this benefit
- dependencies on other parts of the programme, or on risks
- individual responsible for ensuring the successful realisation of the benefit.

Each benefit should relate back to the programme's strategic objectives. If a benefit cannot demonstrate linkage to strategic objectives, even an indirect link, it should be discarded. Note that some benefits are 'enabling' - that is, they are not strategic in themselves but enable other benefits to be realised.

Benefit Profiles must pass four essential tests:
- describing exactly what the benefit is
- providing a measurable comparison between pre and post programme implementation
- describing where the benefit will arise
- describing how the benefit will be measured.

12.5 Identifying the stakeholders

The stakeholder groups and their various needs should be identified, together with plans for communications with each group. There may be stakeholders who will resist the change and/or be disadvantaged by its outcomes. It is particularly important to take account of these stakeholders, as their interaction with the programme could have a serious impact.

12.6 Determining the Project Portfolio and tranches

The Project Portfolio must contain:
- a detailed description of each project
- its dependencies with other projects
- its contribution to benefit realisation.

A programme is almost always delivered in tranches rather than in one phase. Project delivery is scheduled to coincide with delivery of benefits, with a review point at the end of each tranche of projects. Each review point provides the opportunity to rescope subsequent projects if required.

12.7 Developing the programme's organisation structure

The programme organisation must be aligned with the established structure of the parent organisation. The size and nature of the programme will dictate the design of its organisation structure. Each individual should be allocated to an appropriate role within the organisation structure, based on their skills and experience.
Sufficient time and resources needs to be set aside for procurement and contract management activities, as these can take a considerable amount of time.

12.8 Developing the programme's Business Case

It is important to provide as much information as possible in the Business Case at this point, as well as providing confidence in the estimates to give a clearer understanding of the benefits, costs and risks that may arise during the programme.

12.9 Developing the programme's governance arrangements

Governance arrangements must cover how the programme will juggle the inevitable interdependencies as well as bringing all the different components of the programme together. The key strategies are:
- benefits management
- stakeholder management
- risk management and issue resolution
- quality management
- planning and control
- resource management.

12.10 Developing the Benefits Realisation Plan

The Benefits Realisation Plan must ensure that the benefits will be achievable. It should identify opportunities for 'quick wins' if possible, to obtain early stakeholder commitment to the change.

12.11 Developing the Programme Plan

Key information that makes up the Programme Plan is concerned with details of the projects in the portfolio, the resources required and the expected timescales, together with plans for tracking progress and controlling the programme. Initially this information will be indicative only; it will be updated as more accurate information becomes available. The broad timetable for project delivery is produced at this stage, showing how the projects and benefits will be structured as tranches.

12.12 Approval to proceed

The programme owner should approve detailed documentation about the programme (governance, plans and Business Case) before sign-off by the Sponsoring Group at a formal review.

Summary of programme information for this process	
Blueprint	refined
Business Case	created
Programme organisation	created
Project Portfolio	created
Benefit Profiles	created
Stakeholder Map	created
Programme Planning and Control	created
Resource Management Strategy	created
Benefits Management Strategy	created
Stakeholder Management Strategy	created
Risk Management Strategy	created
Issue Resolution Strategy	created
Quality Management Strategy	created
Programme Plan	created
Benefits Realisation Plan	created
Communications Plan	created
Risk Register	created
Issue Log	created

Table 12.1 *Summary of programme information for* Defining a programme

CHAPTER 13

Governing a programme

13.1 Introduction

Governing a programme puts in place the governance arrangements that will determine how the programme is set up, managed and controlled.
This section outlines how the governance arrangements underpin programme delivery.

13.2 Setting up the programme organisation

Programme organisation set-up consists of the appropriate individuals being formally appointed. Skills must be defined and competencies must be assessed to determine suitability for the roles required. It is important that individuals understand and accept the roles and responsibilities to which they have been appointed, together with their reporting lines.

13.3 Setting up the Programme Office

The Programme Office provides an 'information hub' for the programme throughout its life. Depending on the scale of the programme, there may be a team of people providing programme support or just one individual. The Programme Office is set up by determining:
- what information will be needed to support decision making for the programme
- how to ensure consistency in data collection and reporting
- how to ensure easy access to stored information.

13.4 Supporting governance requirements

Funding arrangements need to be agreed and the accounting procedures implemented. The approach to handling risks and issues and reporting arrangements must be consistent at both programme and project level.

13.5 Setting up the physical programme environment

Resources relating to the physical environment of the programme such as buildings and equipment need to be identified and established, along with the IT infrastructure.

13.6 Risk management and issue resolution

It is critical that the programme's Risk Management Strategy is continually monitored and reviewed, to enable the programme to be aware of any changes in the programme that may become a risk. The Risk Register is updated, with full details of all the main risks to the programme, their owners and plans for managing each risk. The Issues Log is similarly updated.

13.7 HR management

If there are major changes to be introduced through new ways of working, input will be required from the organisation's HR experts. Their advice may be needed on issues such as retraining and consultation with trade unions.

13.8 Procurement and contract management

Procurement and contract management arrangements must be incorporated into corporate policies and standards that may be adjusted to meet the requirements of the programme. If procurement/legal/contract expertise is likely to be required, appropriate sources of expertise need to be identified at this stage.

13.9 Programme communications

The programme's communications channels to the various stakeholders are defined in the Communications Plan. Its main purpose is to ensure that all stakeholder groups are informed about their interests throughout the life of the programme.

13.10 Reporting, monitoring and control

Any issues that arise must be reported and dealt with promptly to enable the programme to stay on target.

It is important that information is updated, refined and maintained at the end of each tranche. This should be reflected in the Programme Plan and the Benefits Realisation Plan.

13.11 Information management

The Programme Office updates the programme's information throughout the life of the programme. Key documents that must be maintained constantly are the Programme Plan and the Benefits Realisation Plan.

13.12 End-of-tranche reviews

All benefits should be reviewed for their delivery (or, conversely, their non-delivery) at the end of each tranche. The findings of each of the reviews should be disseminated to the programme's stakeholders and corrective action taken if benefits have not been achieved in line with plans.

There should be at least one review after the programme has closed to assess benefits realisation after programme completion.

13.13 Maintaining 'business as usual'

Existing business operations will need to continue, as the programme will rely on the organisation's systems and services throughout the process of transition to new ways of working. There will also need to be appropriate actions taken to minimise disruption to the organisation while the change(s) is taking place.

Summary of programme information for this process	
Blueprint	refined
Business Case	refined
Programme organisation	implemented
Project Portfolio	refined
Benefit Profiles	refined
Stakeholder Map	refined
Programme Planning and Control	implemented
Resource Management Strategy	implemented
Benefits Management Strategy	implemented
Stakeholder Management Strategy	implemented
Risk Management Strategy	implemented
Issue Resolution Strategy	implemented
Quality Management Strategy	implemented
Programme Plan	refined
Benefits Realisation Plan	refined
Communications Plan	refined
Risk Register	updated
Issue Log	updated

Table 13.1 *Summary of programme information for* Governing a programme

CHAPTER 14

Managing the portfolio

14.1 Introduction

Managing the portfolio involves coordinating and managing delivery from the projects in the Project Portfolio. This is the responsibility of the Programme Manager. These activities are repeated for each tranche of the programme and need to be aligned to the *Managing benefits* process.

14.2 Project start-ups

The Programme Manager commissions projects in the Project Portfolio. It is essential that each project management team fully understands the content of their Project Brief before their project begins. It must describe a clear scope and measurable definition of the required outcomes. Project management standards must be in place to get the project successfully off the ground.

The Project Brief should include:
- the Project Definition
- a project-level Business Case
- a timetable for delivery
- quality criteria for deliverables
- the main risks identified.

14.3 Project and programme objectives

Some projects may already be underway; others will start later in the programme. The objectives of each project must be aligned with those of the programme; some projects may need rescoping if the programme direction changes.

14.4 Benefits realisation

The Business Change Manager role checks that the benefits expected from each project are realistic and can be achieved.

14.5 Monitoring progress

Monitoring progress should be a continuous activity throughout the programme, carried out by the Programme Office. Project reporting should provide highlight information in a common format to help coordinate key information at programme level. The key areas to monitor are:

- the outputs continuing to meet the programme's objectives and contributing as expected to benefits realisation
- delivery on time and to budget
- changes to risks, issues and assumptions and/or to scope
- accuracy of estimates (evidence based wherever possible).

14.6 Managing risks and resolving issues

Risks and issues need to be identified, reported, escalated and resolved as early as possible.

14.7 Project closure

Project outputs must be formally handed over to the programme when each project is concluded. The process of project closure should include the communication of lessons learned, to share knowledge and experiences with the remaining projects, for the benefit of the programme as a whole.

14.8 Managing stakeholders

Gaining stakeholder cooperation and commitment is critical for the success of the programme. The Communications Plan is the main source of information for managing stakeholders; it should include plans for dealing with conflicting interests in different stakeholder groups as well as plans for overcoming resistance to the change.

Summary of programme information for this process	
Blueprint	updated
Business Case	reviewed
Project Portfolio	refined
Benefit Profiles	refined
Stakeholder Map	refined
Programme Planning and Control	refined
Resource Management Strategy	refined
Benefits Management Strategy	refined
Stakeholder Management Strategy	refined
Risk Management Strategy	refined
Issue Resolution Strategy	refined
Quality Management Strategy	refined
Programme Plan	updated
Benefits Realisation Plan	updated
Communications Plan	updated
Risk Register	updated
Issue Log	updated

Table 14.1 *Summary of programme information for* Managing the portfolio

CHAPTER 15

Managing benefits

15.1 Introduction

This process is concerned with tracking benefits throughout their lifecycle, from identification and scoping through to their realisation and measurement. The process also involves managing the transition to new ways of working. This section outlines the main activities for managing benefits.

15.2 Establishing benefits measurements

In order to make a full assessment of benefit realisation, there needs to be baseline information about how things were before the programme began. Without this there will be no way of measuring if the benefits have made an improvement or not.

15.3 Refining Benefits Profiles

Benefits Profiles are managed in the same way as budgets, to ensure that the expected benefits are still achievable and to identify opportunities for further benefits. (With budget management there are expectations about how much funding is needed; there are also continual checks for opportunities to stretch budgets further - or at least to avoid the risk of overrunning budget estimates.) The Benefits Profiles are continually updated to reflect any changing expectations about benefits delivery.

15.4 Benefits monitoring

Actual progress against expected benefits delivery is tracked against the assumptions in the Business Case, Programme Plan, Benefits Realisation Plan and Blueprint.

15.5 Transition management

As each project nears completion, the relevant business operations need to be ready for implementation of the outputs from the projects.
The transition plan should provide the route map for implementation.

15.6 Managing the cultural aspects

Cultural aspects are usually the most critical factor for success in a change programme. Those most affected by the change will need to be supported in adapting to new ways of working. Training programmes, events such as roadshows and the involvement of HR professionals may all be required.

15.7 Supporting benefit realisation

It is the responsibility of the Business Change Manager to provide ongoing support throughout the programme.

15.8 Measuring benefits

Measuring benefit realisation should be part of the end-of-tranche reviews.

Summary of programme information for this process	
Vision Statement	reviewed
Blueprint	updated
Business Case	reviewed
Project Portfolio	refined
Benefit Profiles	updated
Stakeholder Map	refined
Programme Planning and Control	refined
Resource Management Strategy	refined
Benefits Management Strategy	refined
Stakeholder Management Strategy	refined
Risk Management Strategy	refined
Issue Resolution Strategy	refined
Quality Management Strategy	refined
Programme Plan	updated
Benefits Realisation Plan	updated
Communications Plan	updated
Risk Register	updated
Issue Log	updated

Table 15.1 *Summary of programme information for* Managing benefits

CHAPTER 16

Closing a programme

16.1 Introduction

Programmes should be brought to a formal close when all the projects have delivered their planned outputs into the programme and benefits are being realised from the change. Success (or otherwise) is measured in a final review of the outcomes achieved. This section outlines the activities involved in bringing the programme to a formal conclusion.

16.2 Confirming programme closure

It is essential that the changes brought about by the programme are successfully incorporated into new 'business as usual' operations and working practices of the organisation.

16.3 Programme review

The success of the programme must be reviewed to establish that the Blueprint has been delivered and benefits realised as expected. The review should also include any lesson learned as well as an assessment of the overall performance of the programme and its management.

16.4 Updating and finalising programme information

All information relating to the programme is reviewed and updated, confirming that any outstanding risks and issues have been successfully resolved.

The stakeholders must be informed of programme closure and the realisation of its benefits.

16.5 Disbanding the programme team

The programme team is redeployed back into the parent organisation and the Programme Office closed. If there are contractual arrangements in place, these will need to be formally handed over to the appropriate business area.

16.6 Celebrating success

Finally, it is good practice - and invariably well received by stakeholders - to celebrate the success of the programme. This might be a formal launch, a press announcement or simply an informal event to thank all those involved in the programme's activities.

Summary of programme information for this process	
Vision Statement	reviewed
Blueprint	reviewed
Business Case	reviewed
Programme organisation	reviewed
Project Portfolio	reviewed
Benefit Profiles	reviewed
Stakeholder Map	reviewed
Programme Planning and Control	reviewed
Resource Management Strategy	reviewed
Benefits Management Strategy	reviewed
Stakeholder Management Strategy	reviewed
Risk Management Strategy	reviewed
Issue Resolution Strategy	reviewed
Quality Management Strategy	reviewed
Programme Plan	reviewed
Benefits Realisation Plan	reviewed
Communications Plan	reviewed
Risk Register	reviewed
Issue Log	reviewed

Table 16.1 *Summary of programme information for* Closing a programme

APPENDIX A
Glossary of terms

This glossary includes terms introduced within this guide and others that are relevant to programme management. Many of these terms are also used in a more general sense; the definitions included here are the specific ones used within the discipline of programme management.

assurance	Independent assessment and confirmation that the programme as a whole or any of its aspects are on track, applying relevant practices and procedures, and that the projects, activities and business rationale remain aligned to the programme's objectives
benefit	The quantifiable and measurable improvement resulting from an outcome which is perceived as positive by a stakeholder and which will normally have a tangible value expressed in monetary or resource terms. Benefits are expected when a change is conceived. Benefits are realised as a result of activities undertaken to effect the change
Benefit Profile	The complete description of a benefit or dis-benefit
Benefits Realisation Plan	A complete view of all the Benefit Profiles in the form of a schedule
benefits management	A continuous management process running throughout the programme. It provides the programme with a target and a means of monitoring achievement against that target on a regular basis
Benefits Management Strategy	How the programme will handle benefits management
Blueprint	A model of the business or organisation, its working practices and processes, the information it requires and the technology that will be needed to deliver the capability described in the Vision Statement
Business Case	A document aggregating the specific programme information on overall costs, the anticipated benefit realisation, the timeframe, and the risk profile of the programme
Business Case Management	The manner in which the programme's rationale, objectives, benefits and risks are balanced against the financial investment, and this balance maintained, adjusted and assessed during the programme
Business Change Manager	The role responsible for benefits management, from identification through to delivery, and ensuring the implementation and embedding of the new capabilities delivered by the projects. Typically allocated to more than one individual. Alternative title: 'Change Agent'
capability	A service, function or operation that enables the organisation to exploit opportunities
Change Agent	See Business Change Manager
Communications Plan	A plan of the communications activities during the programme

cross-organisational programme	A programme requiring the committed involvement of more than one organisation to achieve the desired outcomes. Also referred to as 'cross-cutting' programmes
dependency network	A representation of all the inputs and outputs from the projects and how they interrelate, treating each project as a 'black box'
dis-benefit	An unwanted result of an outcome; the negative quantification of an outcome
end goal	The ultimate objective of a programme
Gateway Review	A formal and independent review of the programme (or project) providing assurance on whether the programme is operating effectively and is likely to achieve its outcomes
governance (as used in this guide)	The functions, responsibilities, processes and procedures that define how the programme is set up, managed and controlled
issue	A problem, query, concern or change request that affects the programme and requires management intervention and action to resolve
Issue Log	The log of all issues raised during the programme
Issue Resolution Strategy	How the programme will handle issue resolution
outcome	The result of change, normally affecting real-world behaviour and/or circumstances. Outcomes are desired when a change is conceived. Outcomes are achieved as a result of the activities undertaken to effect the change
portfolio management	The co-ordination of a number of projects
product	Any input or output that can be identified and described in a tangible or measurable way
programme	A portfolio of projects and activities that are co-ordinated and managed as a unit such that they achieve outcomes and realise benefits
Programme Board	A group or committee that may be established to assist with the direction-setting and leadership of a programme. The Sponsoring Group may form a Programme Board
Programme Brief	An outline description of the programme's objectives, desired benefits, risks, costs and timeframe
programme definition	The collection of information defining the programme covering: Vision Statement, Blueprint, Business Case, organisation structure, Project Portfolio, Benefit Profiles, Stakeholder Map
Programme Director	The title previously used for the role with ultimate accountability for the programme - 'Senior Responsible Owner' is the title used in this guide
programme management	The co-ordinated organisation, direction and implementation of a portfolio of projects and activities that together achieve outcomes and realise benefits that are of strategic importance
Programme Manager	The role responsible for the set-up, management and delivery of the programme. Typically allocated to a single individual
Programme Mandate	The trigger for the programme from senior management who are sponsoring the programme
Programme Office	The function providing the information hub for the programme and its delivery objectives

programme organisation	How the programme will be managed throughout its lifecycle, the roles and responsibilities of individuals involved in the programme, and personnel management or Human Resources arrangements
Programme Plan	A comprehensive document scheduling the projects, their costs, resources, risks, and transition activities together with monitoring and control activities
project	A particular way of managing activities to deliver specific outputs over a specified period and within cost, quality and resource constraints
Project Portfolio	A list of all the projects and activities that together will deliver the required 'future state' described in the Blueprint and hence achieve the capabilities expressed in the Vision Statement
Quality Management Strategy	How the programme will achieve the required levels of quality in the way the programme is managed and directed, and how the programme's deliverables will be assessed for 'fitness for purpose'
Resource Management Strategy	Description of the resource requirements for the programme and how they will be managed
Risk	A negative threat (or potential positive opportunity) that might affect the course of the programme
Risk Log	See Risk Register
Risk Management Strategy	How the programme will establish and maintain an effective risk management regime on the programme
Risk Register	The log of all risks identified during the programme. Often called the 'Risk Log'
role	A particular set of responsibilities and accountabilities that may be allocated to one or more individuals. In some circumstances, roles may be merged together as long as there is no conflict of interest
Senior Responsible Owner	The title given to the individual who is ultimately accountable for successful delivery, that is, the successful achievement of desired outcomes and realisation of expected benefits from a programme. This role was previously referred to as 'Programme Director'
Sponsoring Group	Senior level sponsorship of the programme providing the investment decision and top-level endorsement of the rationale and objectives for the programme. May be known as 'Programme Board'
stakeholder	An individual, group of organisation with an interest in, or influence over, the programme
Stakeholder Management	How the programme will identify and analyse the stakeholders and how ongoing communications will be achieved between the programme and all its stakeholders
Strategy	A matrix showing stakeholders and their particular interests in the programme
Stakeholder Map tranche	A group of projects structured around distinct step changes in capability and benefit delivery
value management	A management technique to define the perceived and actual value to the organisation, and then assessing progress and achievements based on this value
Vision Statement	An outward-facing description of the new capabilities resulting from programme delivery

APPENDIX B

Programme documents

- Benefits Profile
- Benefits Realisation Plan
- Benefits Management Strategy
- Blueprint
- Business Case (for the programme)
- Communications Plan
- Issue Log
- Issue Resolution Strategy
- Programme Brief
- Programme Mandate
- Programme Plan
- Project Portfolio
- Quality Management Strategy
- Resource Management Strategy
- Risk Management Strategy
- Risk Register
- Stakeholder Management Strategy
- Stakeholder Map
- Vision Statement

B1: Benefits Profile

Purpose: Used to define each benefit (and dis-benefit) and track its realisation
Outline of contents:
- Description of the benefit (or dis-benefit)
- Interdependencies with other benefits
- When the benefit is expected to occur and over what period of time realisation will take place
- Measure for the realisation of the benefit and how it will be carried out; the 'before' state measurement; financial valuations wherever possible
- Key performance indicators in the business operations that will be affected by the benefit, immediately after realisation and for the future, and current or baseline per-

formance levels. This may be achieved through the measurement of a single benefit or of a group of benefits
- Details of the changes required to the current business processes and operations in order for the benefit to be realised
- Costs associated with realisation and measurement
- Project(s) within the programme directly related to the realisation of the benefit
- Any dependencies on risks or other programmes or projects
- Individual responsible for realisation of the benefit and who will 'own' the Benefit Profile during the programme. This will typically be the relevant Business Change Manager appointed from the business area concerned

B2: Benefits Realisation Plan

Purpose: Used to track realisation of benefits across the programme
Outline of contents:
- Schedule detailing when each benefit or group of benefits will be realised
- Identification of appropriate milestones when a programme benefit review could be carried out
- Details of any handover activities, beyond the mere implementation of a deliverable or output, to sustain the process of benefits realisation after the programme is closed

B3: Benefits Management Strategy

Purpose: Used to establish the approach to managing benefits
Outline of contents:
- Outline description of the programme's benefits and where in the organisation the benefits will occur
- Model of the benefits showing any interdependencies and dependencies on specific areas of change required within the organisation
- Description of the functions, roles and responsibilities for benefit planning and realisation, aligned with the programme's organisation structure
- Review and assessment process for measuring benefit realisation covering: who will be involved in the reviews; how and when the reviews will be carried out

B4: Blueprint

Purpose: Used to maintain the programme's focus on delivering the required transformation and business change

Outline of contents:

- Business models of functions, processes and operations, including operational costs and performance levels, of the required 'future' state
- Organisation structure, staffing levels, roles and skill requirements necessary to support the future business operations. Any necessary changes to organisational culture, style, or existing structures and personnel may also be included
- Technology, IT systems, tools, equipment, buildings and accommodation required for the future business operations together with details of reuse of existing infrastructure or implementation of new infrastructure to support the 'future' state
- Data and information required for the future business operations, together with details of how existing data and information will be changed or redeveloped to provide the necessary requirements for the 'future' state

B5: Business Case (for the programme)

Purpose: Used to validate the ongoing viability of the programme

Outline of contents:

- Strategic objectives for the programme, reflecting the Vision Statement, and alignment with the organisational context and business environment
- Expected benefits or outcomes, with recognition of the organisation's capability to achieve the necessary transformation and change
- Overall risk profile, indicating the major risks to programme delivery and benefit realisation. Detailed risk assessment will be part of the programme's Risk Register
- Any assumptions that underpin the Business Case
- Estimated costs and overall timescales. Detailed scheduling of programme milestones will be part of the Programme Plan
- Investment appraisal (if appropriate)

B6:   Communications Plan

Purpose: Used to plan and monitor the communication activities during the programme

Outline of contents:
- Description of key messages and programme information to be communicated, and the objectives for delivering these communications
- Responsibilities for delivering key messages and other information about the programme
- Description of channels to be used
- Schedule of communications activities, including target audiences for each

B7:   Issue Log

Purpose: Used to capture and actively manage programme issues

Outline of contents:
- Unique reference for each issue raised, date it was raised and by whom
- Description of the issue and what actual or likely impact it has on the programme or projects
- The severity of the issue, for example, the degree to which the interests of the programme could be harmed. Categories for severity might be 'critical' (that is, adverse effect on the benefits such that continuation of the programme is unacceptable), 'major', 'significant', and 'minor'
- Programme Manager has overall responsibility for resolving issues, however, each issue should be assigned to an individual who is best placed to take or manage the necessary actions
- Current status of the issue and progress on its resolution including providing feedback to the source

B8:   Issue Resolution Strategy

Purpose: Used to implement appropriate mechanisms and procedures for resolving issues

Outline of contents:
- How issues will be captured and assessed, and by whom
- How information about their likely impact will be defined
- How ownership will be handled

- How actions will be identified and by whom; who will carry out and manage the required actions
- How actions will be monitored and evaluated for their effectiveness
- What communication mechanisms will be set up; how stakeholders will be engaged throughout the process

B9: Programme Brief

Purpose: Used to define the programme objectives and outcomes
Outline of contents:
- Description of the capability the organisation seeks from changes to the business and/or its operations. Delivery of this capability is the end goal of the programme. The description forms an outline Vision Statement for the programme.
- Outline description of the benefits or types of benefits that should be delivered from the new capability, an estimate of when they are likely to be achieved, and an indication of how they will be measured. It is often necessary to consider 'dis-benefits' (where one of the parties may be worse off as a result of the programme) alongside the benefits in order to present a more complete and realistic 'picture' of the programme's outcome
- Explanation of the risks to the programme that can be recognised at this point in time, any current issues that may affect the programme, and any known constraints, assumptions or conflicts that may potentially affect the programme. It is important to be able to balance the desired benefits arising from the programme against the risks and issues that may prevent the benefits from being fully realised
- As much detail as is available on the estimated costs, timescales and effort required to set up, manage and run the programme from start-up through to delivery and realisation of the benefits. The overall timescale for the programme may be relatively long, perhaps two to five years. To provide an indication of the effort and resources required, an initial listing of candidate projects or activities required should be included, together with rough timescales

B10: Programme Mandate

Purpose: Used to describe the required outcomes from the programme based on strategic or policy objectives

Outline of contents:
- What the programme is intended to deliver in terms of new services and/or operational capability
- How the organisation(s) involved will be improved as a result of delivering the new services/capability
- How the programme fits into the corporate mission and goals and any other initiatives that are already underway or will be underway during the lifetime of the programme

B11: Programme Plan

Purpose: Used to design the overall programme and then to monitor and control progress

Outline of contents:
- Project information including the list of projects (the Project Portfolio), their target timescales and costs, and the dependency network showing the dependencies between the projects
- Summary of the risks and assumptions identified against successful achievement of the Programme Plan. The programme's Risk Register contains the detailed risk assessment and associated contingency actions
- Overall programme schedule showing the relative sequencing of the projects, the grouping of projects into tranches, milestone review points. The schedule should also include timings of communications activities, risk mitigation actions and quality review work to be carried out at the programme level
- Transition plan showing when the outputs from the projects will be delivered to the business and what transition activities will be required to embed the new capability into business operations. The transition plan will need to be closely linked to the programme schedule to ensure any changes in the delivery from the projects is fed into the transition planning process
- Monitoring and control activities, data requirements, performance targets, and responsibilities

B12: Project portfolio

Purpose: Used to define how the programme will deliver the outcome(s) and benefits
Outline of contents:
- List of existing and new projects, together with any relevant workstream activity

- Outline information on outputs, timescales, resource requirements and dependencies with other projects
- Links showing what contribution each project will make to the benefits

B13: Quality Management Strategy

Purpose: Used to define and establish the activities for managing quality across the programme
Outline of contents:
- Description of the quality assurance, review and control processes for the programme covering:
- What will be subject to quality assurance, review and control and the quality criteria to be applied
- Who will undertake quality assurance, review and control activities
- What will trigger these activities (time-based, event-based, or associated with risk occurrence)
- What actions will be taken depending on the results of quality checks
- Configuration Management and change control procedures
- Defined responsibilities for quality management
- Information requirements to support quality management
- Procedures for use of support tools for quality management activities, for example, change control software
- Resource requirements for quality management

B14: Resource Management Strategy

Purpose: Used to identify the required resources and define how they will be acquired and managed
Outline of contents:
- Funding requirements; accounting procedures for costs and expenditure; budgets for programme management resources and funding sources
- Cost and expenditure profile across the programme; expenditure approval procedures; financial reporting procedures
- Assets required, such as buildings and office equipment
- Staff and personnel requirements, including HR requirements for supporting staff through transition
- Technology and services required

- Profile of resources that are shared across more than one of the projects within the portfolio. This profile should indicate the expected use by each project of the shared resource within time periods

B15: Risk Management Strategy

Purpose: Used to define and establish the required activities and responsibilities for managing the programme's risks

Outline of contents:
- How risks will be identified and quantified
- How information about their probability and impact will be defined
- How risk ownership will be handled
- How responses and actions will be identified
- How decisions on risk management will be made, and by whom, for example, tolerance levels
- How these decisions will be implemented
- How actions will be monitored and evaluated for their effectiveness
- What communication mechanisms will be set up, how stakeholders will be engaged throughout the process

B16: Risk Register

Purpose: Used to capture and actively manage the programme risks

Outline of contents:
- Unique reference for each risk identified. This reference may need to be reflected in project-level Risk Registers when the risk could impact on one or more projects as well as the programme
- Description of the risk to the programme and which projects are likely to have an impact on the risk (either increasing its likelihood, or reducing it)
- Description of the impact on the programme should the risk materialise
- Proximity of the risk, which is an estimation of timescale for when the risk might materialise. The accuracy of this estimation increases as the point in time approaches. The scale should provide for continuous and equal time windows that will align easily with the programme's risk management processes. For example, if the programme has a planned duration of thirty months and the programme management team has agreed to meet every three months, then the proximity scale could sensibly use three-month increments

- Probability of realisation of the risk. This could be a mathematical calculation, or a simpler 'high, medium, low' classification
- Severity of the risk, for example the degree to which the interests of the programme would be harmed should the risk materialise. Categories for severity might be 'critical' (that is, adverse effect on the benefits such that continuation of the programme is unacceptable), 'major', 'significant', and 'minor'
- Risk owner - the Programme Manager has overall responsibility for managing programme risks; however, each risk should be assigned to the individual who is best placed to monitor it and manage any necessary actions
- Response to the risk, which reduces either the probability of the risk happening or its effects, should it happen
- Current status of the risk itself and progress of any actions relating to the management of the risk

B17: Stakeholder Management Strategy

Purpose: Used to define and implement the objectives, activities and responsibilities for managing stakeholders

Outline of contents:
- List of all stakeholders, appropriately grouped
- Analysis of influence and impact for each stakeholder group
- Stakeholder Map showing the different stakeholder interests in the programme
- Description of how the programme will engage with all stakeholders including mechanisms for encouraging, receiving and responding to feedback from stakeholders
- Measures to determine how well the communication process is engaging with stakeholders

B18: Stakeholder Map

Purpose: Used to model stakeholder interests

Outline of contents:
- Matrix showing each stakeholder or stakeholder group against their interest areas in the programme

B19: Vision Statement

Purpose: Used to communicate the end goal of the programme
Outline of contents:
- Clear statement of the 'end goal' of the programme
- Supported by a description of the new or changed capabilities together with performance measures or service levels indicating the desired improvements resulting from programme delivery

APPENDIX C

Programmes and projects

A project usually has definite start and finish points, with the aim of delivering a predetermined output and a clear development paths from initiation to delivery. A programme has a more strategic vision of the desired end goal, but no clearly defined path to get there. Programmes are able to deal with the uncertainty surrounding the achievement of the vision, whereas projects work best where the outputs can be well defined.

Programmes are about managing change, almost always changes to culture and work practices as well as changes to business operations and services. Changing cultures and styles of management takes time. Programmes can embrace the management and leadership of culture change because they have longer timeframes than projects.

Benefits accrue at the end of a project, after the output has been delivered. In contrast, a programme will co-ordinate the delivery from a set of projects such that benefits can be realised within the timescales of the programme as well as afterwards. A programme is likely to include some projects that do not directly produce benefits but are nonetheless essential to delivering the overall programme benefits.

Relative timescales are also a way of differentiating between a project and a programme. Projects have a shorter timeframe for completion than programmes. Projects will usually be measured in months; programmes will often be measured in years.

The ways in which projects and programmes are managed also demonstrate that a project is different from a programme. Some typical differences between managing project delivery and managing programmes are shown table C.1.

Managing project delivery	Managing programmes
An intense and focused activity that is concerned with delivering predetermined outputs	A broadly spread activity concerned with delivering business change objectives and achieving outcomes, realising a wider set of benefits than the individual projects could realise in isolation
Best suited to closely bounded and scoped deliverables that can be relatively well defined	Suited to activities with complex and changing inter-relationships in a wider, more dynamic and uncertain environment
Realises benefits following the end of the project, after implementation of the project's outputs	Realises benefits both during and after conclusion of the programme, having put in place mechanisms for measuring the improvements in business performance Suited to managing benefits realisation and ensuring a smooth and risk-reduced transition into a new business operation Able to maintain 'business as usual' in areas affected by the change whilst managing the transition to new operations Usually continues until the organisation has achieved the required outcomes (a programme may of course be stopped earlier if it is no longer valid)

Table C.1 *Typical differences between projects and programmes*